CONTINENTAL TRACTION

JAMIE ANDERSON

First published 2021

Amberley Publishing
The Hill, Stroud
Gloucestershire, GL5 4EP

www.amberley-books.com

ISBN 978 1 3981 0681 9 (print)
ISBN 978 1 3981 0682 6 (ebook)

British Library Cataloguing in Publication Data.
A catalogue record for this book is available from the British Library.

Origination by Amberley Publishing.
Printed in the UK.

Introduction

I suppose you could say railways are in my blood – my mother's father was a lifelong employee of the enormous GWR works at Swindon. No doubt his working day was spent around the various Castles, Halls and Kings and in later years the likes of No. 92220 *Evening Star*, the last steam locomotive built for British Rail. My Auntie is currently working for Network Rail and formed part of the team that contributed to the electrification of the Great Western mainline. As a young boy I remember my parents taking me to Swindon station to watch the various passenger and freight workings coming and going, including the High Speed Trains arriving from or heading to London Paddington. The spark was lit and after a house move in Swindon brought me closer to the railway a few years ago, that spark has since turned into a roaring passion for the railways. Since 2017 I have explored the rail network of the United Kingdom, visiting everywhere from Penzance to Edinburgh and Ipswich to Carmarthen, and plenty of locations in between. On all these adventures my trusty Fujifilm FinePix S3400 digital camera has been by my side, and this was used to capture every picture you will see in this book.

As my passion for the railways grew and grew, my attentions inevitably started to turn towards the rail network of the Continent. My first excursion across the English Channel occurred in July 2015. The holiday itself was a week-long coach tour of the Alps, and while in Switzerland I travelled the Chur to Arosa line and photographed my first piece of Continental traction in the shape of Rhatische Bahn ABe 8/12 No. 3501, which carried the name *Willem Jan Holsboer*. My next encounter with the European rail network occurred in February 2016 while on an Arctic cruise of Norway, where I photographed NSB Class BM 93 No. 58 at Andalsnes. This took me and some fellow cruise passengers on the Rauma Railway from Andalsnes to Dombas – the snow was thick on the ground and the scenery was incredible. I was well and truly hooked on the Continental rail network. My first full rail holiday took place during September 2017, where I spent two weeks in Switzerland. During this holiday I rode on the Pilatus Bahn as well as the Golden Pass line, with the highlight of the holiday being the chance to ride on the Jungfraubahn from Lauterbrunnen, changing at Kleine Scheidegg to reach the Jungfraujoch. This is Europe's highest railway station, at a height of 11,332 feet. The line itself is an engineering and railway wonder that runs through the mountain cores of the Eiger and Monch before finishing on the mountain saddle that sits between the Monch and Jungfrau mountains, where the high-altitude station is located. It was on this trip to Switzerland that I met my good friend and fellow rail enthusiast Diane Taylor, who has shared many great adventures with me.

After doing several group tours to the Continent I decided to have a go at a solo holiday visiting Sweden, travelling via northern Germany and Denmark. This allowed me to visit multiple locations in my own time and capture many pictures of Swedish, German and Danish traction. The trip went so well that I later took a two-week holiday exploring southern Germany as well as Hungary, Slovakia, the Czech Republic and Austria. In this book I have aimed to capture as many different classes and forms of traction that are found on the Continent as I could, including the enormous variety of both national and non-national operators on both the freight and passenger workings. By far the most common traction types seen in these pages are the Bombardier TRAXX, the Siemens EuroSprinter and the Siemens Mobility Vectron. These three classes can be found pretty much anywhere and are equally at home on freight diagrams as well as long-distance passenger services and a variety of night train routes. Although all three types have a foothold in Hungary and Slovakia, both countries still maintain large varied fleets of Skoda-built locomotive types, such as the MAV classes 431/2/3 and 630 in Hungary and the ZSSK classes 240 and 361 in Slovakia.

At any moment tons of freight is on the move, covering vast distances on dedicated freight routes across the Continent. Within these pages a large number of freight workings have been photographed conveying a large variety of goods. Among the more usual freight workings, such as intermodal containers and scrap, are more interesting workings such as iron ore and cement. Whereas some types of freight, in particular intermodal workings, can be seen anywhere and everywhere, some freight types are more isolated. These include grain and coal workings in Eastern Europe and iron ore and logs in the far north of Norway. Just as varied as the freight diagrams is the traction that hauls it, and some less common types can be found such as the Ge 6/6 II in Switzerland hauling short rakes of mixed freight and the incredible IORE locomotives hauling heavy iron ore trains from Kiruna to Narvik. The IORE is one of the most powerful locomotives in the world. Another common sight on the Continent at stations and freight yards are the station pilots and shunters, and there is a huge variety here too.

When one thinks of passenger services on the Continent, the mind is immediately drawn towards the high-speed services that whisk passengers over long distances in a short period of time. The most well-known high-speed train services are those operated by the French TGV and German ICE fleets, both of which have various classes – the TGV family has no fewer than nineteen different classes of traction, and the ICE fleet is made up of eight different types of traction. Alongside these more famous fleets are the lesser-known Swedish X2 Class, and Thalys's fleet of PBA and PBKA high-speed trains. Sometimes overlooked are the electric and diesel multiple units that carry passengers on local stopping services. These come in all shapes and sizes, from the DB Class 628 and Mav 426 diesel multiple units to the Electric multiple unit double-deck DB Class 445 and ZSSK Class 671.

I hope that that you will be inspired to visit the Continental rail network and see for yourself the myriad of traction. There is so much to see and photograph, and who knows? One day we may meet on a platform or train somewhere in Europe.

Austria

Austria has a total rail network of around 3,800 miles, of which some 2,180 is electrified with cross-border lines serving all its neighbouring countries. This allows passengers and freight to move easily through not only Austria but the Continent in general. The national operator here is OBB, which uses a varied mix of traction with the Electric Eurosprinter family of locomotives and the older Class 1144 locomotives sharing the loco-hauled passenger and freight duties. Local services are provided by a number of diesel and electric multiple units – the Class 4024 is the most common EMU, and the Class 5047 is the most common DMU.

21 February 2020

OBB Class 1016 No. 010 is seen at Innsbruck while on a passenger working with a rake of single-deck carriages. Just visible in the background is the Innsbruck ski jump and a Class 4024 electric multiple unit.

21 February 2020

OBB Class 1016 No. 014 is at Innsbruck coupled up to a OBB Class 1116 hauling a rake of intermodal wagons. The combination of the snow-capped Alps and 014 displaying an advertising livery for CAT City Airport Train make for a colourful view.

20 February 2020

OBB Class 1016 No. 038 is making a station call at Innsbruck with a passenger working as the last rays of light signal the end of another day. The Class 1016 is a single-voltage type and can be found on freight and passenger workings throughout Austria.

15 July 2018

OBB Class 1116 No. 088 is found at Villach among the rolling Alpine scenery with an interesting working consisting of vans and coaches.

21 February 2020

OBB Class 1116 No. 089 is at Innsbruck working an intermodal train double-headed with OBB Class 1016 No. 014, which can be seen in a previous picture. The pair are waiting for the signal to proceed.

21 February 2020

OBB Class 1116 No. 200 is seen at Innsbruck on a fine sunny afternoon while on a passenger working. This particular example is displaying a very detailed and colourful livery for the Austrian parliament.

20 February 2020

OBB Class 1116 No. 207 is at Innsbruck having just brought the author in from Zurich and is heading on to its destination, Prague. This 1116 belongs to a fifty-nine-strong fleet reserved for and turned out in Railjet livery. The 1116 Class are a dual-voltage type allowing them to work into Hungary/Czech Republic and Switzerland on Railjet services.

21 February 2020

OBB Class 1116 Nos 061 and 194 have just arrived at Innsbruck hauling a double-headed passenger workings. 061 is about to be uncoupled and 194 will take the working further. 061 will proceed out of the station and reverse into the goods yard where it will be stabled.

21 February 2020

OBB Class 1114 No. 40 is found stabled at Innsbruck with a rake of single-deck carriages. The Class 1114 can be found on a variety of passenger and freight workings throughout Austria but are rarely seen on cross-border workings as they are a single-voltage type. Of note is the retro livery.

20 February 2020

OBB Class 1144 No. 042 is making a station call at Innsbruck with a push-pull city shuttle working. Like most of its class, this example is displaying the current OBB livery.

21 February 2020

OBB Class 4024 No. 075 is seen stabled at Innsbruck in the early evening while between passenger duties. The Class 4024 is a single-voltage electric multiple unit and can be found on local workings throughout Austria.

21 February 2020

OBB Class 4024 No. 118 is on a local service departing from Innsbruck at 16.50 and will head to Hall in Tirol, where the service will terminate. A dual-voltage version of this class carrying the class identification of 4124 works cross-border into Slovakia and Hungary.

Croatia

When it formed part of Yugoslavia, Croatia was connected to its neighbours as part of a wider network. However when Yugoslavia collapsed rail lines were torn up, severing cross-border links to other countries. Today's railways are thankfully in better shape. The national operator here is HZ, with a national network of some 1,600 miles of track, of which around 600 is electrified with several cross-border lines. Serving Hungary, Slovenia, Serbia and Bosnia, Class 1141 and 1142 electric locomotives are the backbone of loco-hauled and freight services. Class 7121 and 7122 are the most common DMU types, and Class 6111 is the most common EMU. However, these older types are being phased out in favour of newer stock.

22 May 2018

HZ Class 7122 No. 027 is seen at Split on a warm sunny afternoon having just arrived with a working from Kastel Stari. The Class 7122 are diesel mutiple units that were purchased second-hand from Swedish operator SJ in four batches between 1995 and 2007.

Denmark

With a network of some 1,400 miles, Denmark has several interesting cross-border routes as well as domestic lines. DSB is the national operator here and while the main line from Germany, which goes via Flensburg to Copenhagen and into Sweden, is electrified most other lines are strictly diesel. The Danish loco-hauled services are handled by Class EA and Me, but these are due to be replaced by Vectron locomotives soon. The electric multiple unit of choice is the Class ER, while Diesel Multiple Units are of classes MF MG and MQ. With Copenhagen S Bahn being made up of classes SA and SE, Denmark sees lots of freight passing through between Sweden and Germany. The other route to Germany involves the train going across the sea by rail ferry.

24 February 2019

DSB Class ER No. 2026 is seen arriving at Copenhagen. The ER Class of electric multiple units are numbered 2001–2017 for suburban service and Nos 2018–2044 have a buffet service for longer-distance diagrams.

24 February 2019

DSB Class ER No. 2036 is at Copenhagen with a long-distance service and is about to depart. The ER Class and its diesel counterpart the Class MF are considered ugly by some.

24 February 2019

DSB Class MF No. 5079 is at Copenhagen station as the last passengers board. The Class MF are the diesel multiple unit version of the electric ER Class. These units are found on inter-city services throughout Denmark.

24 February 2019

DSB Class MF No. 5236 is seen making a station call at Copenhagen on a wonderfully sunny, crisp winter's afternoon. Sadly 5236 has recently suffered graffiti damage and has not been fully cleaned.

24 February 2019

DSB Class MG No. 5648 has just arrived at Copenhagen, where the service has terminated upon arrival. The Class MG is a diesel mutiple unit that serves the Copenhagen–Aarhus–Aalborg route.

24 February 2019
DSB Class MG No. 5872 is at Copenhagen heading towards Aalborg and is working in tandem with classmate No. 5821. In the background a DSB Class SA can been seen on an S-Bahn service.

24 February 2019

SJ Class X2K No. 2040 catches the late afternoon sun as it prepares to work from Cophenhagen with a cross-border service to the Swedish capital Stockholm. The dual-voltage X2K and single-voltage X2 classes are high-speed tilting trains that can be found all over Sweden. Only the X2K Class can be found outside Sweden.

France

France has the second largest rail network on the Continent, with roughly 18,000 miles of track. The national operator here is SNCF, which operates a huge variety of locomotives and multiple units – although the most famous fleet of traction is undoubtedly the TGV, of which no fewer than fifteen different classes service both national and international routes. France has excellent connections to its neighbouring countries and the wider Continental network, including the Channel Tunnel that links France and the UK. These services are operated by Eurostar and Le Shuttle.

15 September 2019

SNCF Class BB 26000 No. 26144 is seen at Strasbourg in glorious sunshine with the 12.51 cross-border service to Basel. The Class BB 26000 is a dual-voltage type that can be found working internal services in France as well as cross-border workings. This class are nicknamed sybic.

22 September 2019

SNCF Class BB 26000 No. 26151 has just arrived at Strasbourg from Basel with the 11.39 service. Out of sight at the rear of the carriages, a SNCF shunter has coupled up and will go with 26151 to the carriage depot where the the carriages will undergo cleaning and maintenance.

22 September 2019

SNCF Class Y 8000 No. 8112 has just coupled up to the rear of a passenger service at Strasbourg from Basel. SNCF BB 26000 No. 26151 is on the front and will haul the empty coaches to the depot, where 8112 will shunt the carriages after 26151 uncouples.

14 September 2019

SNCF Class TGV 501 No. 542 shows off its aerodynamic lines having just completed a journey to Paris Est. The TGV 501 Class are known as Reseau and typically work TGV diagrams in the north-east of France, extending into Luxembourg.

14 September 2019

SNCF Class TGV 4701 No. 4713 is illuminated by the sun at Paris Est. The TGV 4701 Class are known as Euro Duplex 3UA and are used on international high-speed services. These TGV are triple-voltage capable and are also double-decked.

Germany

With a rail network covering roughly 25,600 miles of track, of which 12,300 is electrified, Germany has the largest rail network on the Continent. DB is the national operator here alongside various private passenger and freight operators. DB operate a large and interesting variety of traction, including the high-speed ICE fleet and the fleet of Class 101 locos hauling the long-distance services. The most common freight loco is the Class 185. Germany has various connections to its neighbouring countries with services being mainly of the ICE and loco-hauled variety, but also a number of night trains that operate internationally as well as domestic routes.

9 February 2020

DB Class 101 No. 002 has just arrived under the vast roof of Munich HBF with a loco-hauled passenger working. The Class 101 is a very common type and can be found on inter-city and euro city workings and also on fast regional services between Munich and Nuremberg.

8 March 2019
DB Class 112 No. 140 is seen at Hamburg with a rake of double-deck carriages on an express regional service. Hamburg is a good station to see this class; within a very short time Class 112 Nos 147, 153 and 168 also arrived.

10 February 2020
DB Class 120 No. 132 is seen under the lights of Munich station late at night having just brought in the empty coaching stock for the EuroNight 463 Kalman Imre sleeper service to Budapest. At the other end of the night train is classmate No. 143.

10 February 2020

DB Class 143 No. 855 has just arrived at Nuremberg with an S-Bahn working and looks enormous compared to the rake of coaches it is pulling. The Class 143 at Nuremberg share the S-Bahn duties with more modern electric multiple units, making for some interesting sights of the old and the new.

8 March 2019

DB Class 152 No. 051 rumbles through Hamburg-Harburg with a long rake of intermodal wagons destined for the port of Hamburg. With its close proximity to the port, Hamburg-Harburg is a freight hotspot and you can never be sure of what traction and cargo combination will arrive next.

8 March 2019

DB Class 182 No. 019 is seen at Hamburg with a rake of double-deck passenger coaches while working Regional Express No. 1 to Rostock HBF. Only twenty-five of this class are operated by DB and they are very similar to the OBB Class 1116 that is found in Austria.

8 March 2019

DB Class 187 No. 107 passes through Hamburg-Harburg with a rake of intermodal wagons bound for the port of Hamburg. The class 187 entered service in 2016 and is easily recognisable thanks to distinctive side profile area.

8 March 2019

DB Class 261 No. 028 has just pulled into Hamburg-Harburg having travelled from the port area. It will now complete a reversing movement to enter back into the port to continue with shunting duties. Note the autocoupler in yellow attached to the front of No. 028.

9 February 2020

DB Class 362 No. 845 is at Munich acting as a station pilot having just brought in a OBB Class 1216 and the locomotives rake of passenger carriages. No. 845 has just uncoupled and will now return to the yard to await its next turn of duty.

9 February 2020

DB Class 401 No. 069 has just arrived at Munich with an InterCity Express, or ICE for short. The Class 401 is also known as ICE-1, being the first type of dedicated high-speed InterCity Express train sets. No. 069 appears to be carrying a very lengthy scar under the cab side window.

23 February 2019

DB Class 402 No. 236 looks fast even after coming to a stop at Cologne HBF with an ICE working. The Class 402 is also known as ICE-2 and although very similar to the ICE-1, has two powercars instead of one, and a power cab car at the other end.

8 March 2019

DB Class 411 No. 008 has just arrived at Hamburg-Harburg with an ICE working from Hamburg HBF. The Class 411 is known as ICE-T, with the T standing for tilting. A maximum tilt angle of 8 degrees can be achieved by this class.

9 February 2020

DB Class 412 No. 9013 is found at Munich HBF between InterCity Express workings on a cold and sunny winter's morning. The Class 412 is also known as ICE-4 and was built to replace the older ICE-1 and ICE-2 trainsets. Note the unique aerodynamic front end and coupler shape that makes the ICE-4 so distinctive.

9 February 2020

DB Class 445 No. 067 is seen at Munich HBF with a regional working to Nuremberg HBF. The Class 445 was built for double-deck regional workings. This type can be found in pockets around Germany, particularly around Hamburg and Munich.

10 February 2020

DB Class 628 No. 431 makes for an interesting sight at Munich late at night as a diesel multiple unit in a electric-dominated area. The Class 431 were built for regional workings and are now less common – originally 303 were built, but now only 57 remain.

8 February 2020

RailAdventure Class 103 No. 222 is found stabled at Munich HBF along with a Luxon private hire coach which consists of a bar lounge and panorama deck. 222 is the only one of its class owned by RailAdventure, who also operate a number of different types for moving new rolling stock and locomotives to test sites and to their new owners.

23 February 2019

Train Rental GmbH Class 110 No. 428 is found at Cologne stabled next to the station while in between duties. This class is very rare indeed; around 400 were built but only around 25 are still in active service with various operators. Train Rental GmbH own four of them including No. 428.

8 March 2019

Metronom Class 146 No. 14 has just arrived at Hamburg-Harburg with service RB 31, the Hamburg to Luneburg service via Winsen. Metronom operate twenty-nine of this class, with most being named. 14 carries the name *Sarstedt*, which is the name of a town found in the Lower Saxony region of Germany.

10 February 2020

ALEX Class 183 No. 003 is seen at Munich with a short mixed rake of carriages consisting of two single-deck and one double-deck carriage. ALEX operates high-speed express services between Munich and Regensburg using five of this class.

8 March 2019

HSL Logistik GmbH Class 185 No. 600 eases through Hamburg-Harburg on a light engine move. 600 has been on hire to HSL since 2016 from Beacon rail leasing. HSL is an open access freight operator from Hamburg who own or lease various locomotive classes.

8 March 2019

Railpool Class 185 No. 689 runs through Hamburg-Harburg on the way to the port with a load of intermodal wagons destined for locations all over the world. Railpool hire out locomotives to various operators all over the Continent.

8 March 2019

European Locomotive Leasing Class 193 No. 742 trundles slowly through Hamburg-Harburg with a rake of intermodal wagons from the port of Hamburg, destined for the Continent. 742 is looking very smart in the standard ELL livery.

8 March 2019

SBB Cargo International Class 193 No. 209 is nearing journey's end as it passes through Hamburg-Harburg with a colourful rake of intermodal wagons. 209 is a long way from home, normally being based in Switzerland. This loco has been on hire to SBB Cargo International from ELL since 2014.

8 March 2019

Wiener Lokalbahnen Cargo Class 193 No. 224 passes through Hamburg-Harburg on its way from the port of Hamburg with a rake of mostly MSC intermodal wagons. 224 has been on hire to Wiener Lokalbahnen Cargo from ELL since 2015.

8 March 2019

Metronom Class 246 No. 008 has just arrived at Hamburg-Harburg with a rake of double-deck passenger carriages operating RE 5, the Hamburg to Cuxhaven service via Buxtehude and Stade. The Class 246 is the diesel version of the Class 146 seen earlier in this chapter.

9 February 2020

OBB Class 1216 No. 021 is seen at Munich HBF having just been shunted by the station pilot with an international passenger working heading back to Austria. The Class 1216 is a triple-voltage locomotive type allowing them to work into the countries that share borders with Austria on either passenger or freight workings.

9 March 2019

Thalys Class PBKA No. 4307 is seen at Cologne waiting to depart with an international high-speed service to Paris Nord. The PBKA is very similar to the French TGV with the PBKA designation standing for Paris, Brussels, Koln, Amsterdam. These are on the route served by this class.

8 March 2019

Spitzke Logistik GmbH Class V100-SP No. 026 chugs through Hamburg-Harburg with a short rake of auto-ballaster wagons and a single low-sided wagon carrying a wheeled generator. SLG operate a varied fleet that includes small and large shunters as well as heavy freight locomotives.

10 February 2020

SNCF Class TGV 4701 No. 4707 is seen having just arrived at Munich late at night with an international high-speed working from France. Seen in the platform behind 4707 is a DB ICE-3 high-speed train. The two different aerodynamic nose designs make for an interesting comparison.

Hungary

Hungary has a rail network covering some 5,000 miles, of which around 1,900 is electrified. The national operator here is MAV, with the largest private operator being GySEV. Both MAV and GySEV use a variety of locally built locomotives and units, with newer types such as Vectrons and Eurosprinters slowly gaining footholds in the country. The freight operations are handled mainly by Rail Cargo Hungaria, which took over MAV Cargo in 2010 and is owned by OBB. Although lacking any high-speed lines, Hungary has very good connections to its neighbouring countries, including Austria to the west and Ukraine to the east.

12 February 2020

MAV Class 415 No. 110 is found late in the evening at Budapest-Keleti having just arrived with a regional working. Class 415 units are used on various workings out of Budapest. This class is based on the FLIRT electric multiple units, and the old class designation for this type was Class 5341.

12 February 2020

MAV Class 426 No. 028 is seen at Budapest-Keleti waiting to depart with a regional working to Esztergom. The Class 426 is a diesel multiple unit that carried the old class designation of Class 6342. Note the MAV Class 480 that can be seen in the background.

11 February 2020

MAV Class 431 No. 154 is found at Budapest-Keleti with a short rake of three passenger coaches. On the other end is classmate No. 362. Under the old class designation, the Class 431 were Class V43. This type is found all over Hungary on passenger workings.

12 February 2020

MAV Class 432 No. 291 is seen as darkness falls over Budapest-Keleti with a rake of single-deck passenger carriages. The Class 432 are modified versions of the Class 431 with the Class 432 receiving improved suspension as well as a full rebuild. The old designation for this type was Class V43.2.

11 February 2020

MAV Class 433 No. 224 is seen under the roof of Budapest-Keleti on a fine sunny afternoon having just brought in a passenger working. The Class 433 are modified versions of the Class 431 with the Class 433 being fitted with equipment to operate push-pull diagrams. The old designation for this Class was V43.3.

12 February 2020

MAV Class 448 No. 440 is seen at Budapest-Keleti acting as a station pilot and has just shunted a GySEV Class 470 and its rake of carriages into position. The Class 448 used to carry the designation Class M44.4. The Class 448 have in the past undergone full rebuilds and received new diesel engines from Caterpillar.

12 February 2020

MAV Class 460 No. 032 is acting as station pilot at Budapest-Keleti and has just backed onto a rake of now empty passenger carriages and will take them to be serviced and cleaned. The Class 460 carried the old designation Class V46 and this type are used as shunters and on short-distance freight workings. The Class 460 are sometimes referred to as 'HiFi towers'.

11 February 2020

MAV Class 470 No. 001 is seen having just arrived at Budapest-Keleti with a passenger working. The Class 470 carried the old designation Class 1047 and is a dual-voltage type very closely related to the OBB Class 1116, which also belong to the Siemens Eurosprinter family. No. 001 is seen carrying a remembrance livery for the Hungarian Uprising of 1956.

12 February 2020

MAV Class 470 No. 007 prepares to depart from Budapest-Keleti with a short rake of four passenger carriages. No. 007 also displays a special livery for the 52nd International Eucharistic Congress.

12 February 2020

MAV Class 480 No. 004 is found at Budapest-Keleti and is waiting to depart with a rake of single-deck passenger carriages as a railway worker inspects the coupling for the journey ahead. No. 004 is seen here displaying a celebratory livery for the 170th birthday of the Hungarian railway network.

12 February 2020

MAV Class 480 No. 006 is seen at Budapest-Kelenfold with a passenger working destined for Budapest-Keleti. The MAV Class 480 is used on domestic and International passenger trains, which is possible thanks to their dual-voltage capability. No. 006 is seen in a celebratory livery for Szent Marton, Saint Martin, celebrating his 1,700th birthday.

11 February 2020

MAV Class 630 No. 030 makes for a rare sight at Budapest-Keleti as this class normally work only freight diagrams, but is seen here with a passenger service. The old designation for this type was the Class V63 and their nickname is 'Gigant'.

12 February 2020

MAV Class 630 No. 045 is seen at Budapest-Kelenfold as it powers through the station with a rake of empty wagons. Budapest-Kelenfold is located on the outskirts of the city with easy access by rail or metro.

12 February 2020

MVA Class 242 No. 251 has just stopped at Budapest-Kelenfold with a long train of loaded coal wagons. No. 251 will now uncouple and run round its wagons before heading back the way it came in. MVA are an open access freight company based at Debrecen.

13 February 2020

Ceske Drahy Class 380 No. 006 is found at Budapest-Nyugati with the EC 278 service going to Prague via Bratislava. The Class 380 is ideally suited for these types of long-distance international passenger workings thanks to their triple-voltage capability.

12 February 2020

Floyd Class 450 Nos 004 and 008 trundle through Budapest-Kelenfold with a rake of loaded grain wagons. The Class 450 will be instantly recognisable to UK enthusiasts as they served in the UK for many years as Class 86, working passenger and freight workings. These locomotives arrived in Hungary in 2009 with 450-004 being former 86218 and 450-008 being 86242. Floyd also operate a fleet of former Class 56 locos, now reclassed as 659.

12 February 2020

GySEV Class 470 No. 501 is found at Budapest-Keleti late in the evening preparing to depart with a passenger working. 501 is displaying a livery commemorating the Empress of Austria, Elisabeth of Bavaria. She was born on Christmas Eve 1837 and passed away on 10 September 1898, aged sixty.

11 February 2020

GySEV Class 471 No. 005 is seen at Budapest-Keleti waiting to depart with a passenger working consisting of MAV coaches. No. 005 looks very smart and clean, which is the norm for GySEV. The company own six of this class.

12 February 2020

PKP Cargo and Advanced World Transport Class 740 Nos 707 and 674 are seen having just arrived double-headed into the yard next to Budapest-Kelenfold, leading a rake of empty car carriers.

12 February 2020

OBB Class 1116 No. 035 gets underway again after a lengthy stop at Budapest-Kelenfold with a rake of mixed freight. This rake is made up of a cargo wagon, a few covered hoppers and a long rake of box wagons.

12 February 2020

Rail Cargo Hungaria Class 1116 No. 007 gets away from a stopping for a red signal at Budapest-Kelenfold with a rake of cement tanks. Rail Cargo Hungaria is the former MAV Cargo company and was aqquired by OBB in 2010.

12 February 2020

Rail Cargo Hungaria Class 1116 No. 015 crawls light engine into the freight yard next to Budapest-Kelenfold, where it will collect a rake of loaded scrap wagons before heading off to its destination.

Italy

Italy has a large rail network comprising around 10,300 miles of track, of which roughly 8,200 miles have been electrified. Of the electrified track, around 800 miles is on the high-speed lines. The national operator here is Trenitalia, which operate a large mix of traction with the backbone of loco-hauled diagrams in the hands of Class E.402 and the high-speed services being powered by several high-speed types including the Class ETR.400. Italy enjoys a good domestic network as well as international lines into its neighbouring countries, including a link to Switzerland that requires passengers to board the RhB network at Tirano due to a change in the gauge of the track.

17 September 2019

Rhatische Bahn Class ABe 4/4 III No. 52 is seen at Tirano coupled up to classmate No. 54 with a rake of passenger carriages ready for the 15.00 departure to Pontresina. Only six of this class were built and each are named. No. 52 carries the name *Brusio*, which is a municipality in the canton of Grisons. Brusio is also famous for the incredible Brusio spiral viaduct.

17 September 2019

Rhatische Bahn Class ABe 4/4 III No. 54 is at Tirano coupled up to classmate No. 52; as seen in the previous picture. No. 54 is named *Hakone*, which was the first mountain railway in Japan. The full name of the line is the Hakone Tozan Railway.

17 September 2019

Rhatische Bahn Class Ge 2/2 No. 161 rests in the sun at Tirano between station pilot duties. Only two of these fascinating shunters exist, with 161 located at Tirano and 162 at Poschiavo. Although not obvious, this type is very old – they entered service in 1911.

17 September 2019

Trenord Class E.464 No. 413 is found at Tirano with a passenger working, and the Alps make for a wonderful backdrop. Just behind the locomotive is the freight yard at Tirano, which is across from the station. Note the unusual buffers that are fitted to this class.

17 September 2019

Trenord Class ETR.425 No. 031 is seen arriving at Tirano with a regional working for which the class was built. Tirano is a very interesting station. Being so close to the Swiss/Italian border means a good variety of services can be seen at the station.

Norway

With most of its rail network located in the south and south-east of the country, Norway has a network of roughly 2,500 miles of track, of which roughly 1,600 is electrified. The national operator here is Vy, formerly NSB, which handles the passenger workings. The freight side of things is operated by CargoNet. The backbone of loco-hauled workings is the Class El 18, which is very similar to the Swiss Re460. The most common EMU is the BM 75 and the most common DMU is the BM 93. Norway enjoys no fewer than four border crossings to its neighbour Sweden, one of which is the iron ore line that connects the port of Narvik with the Swedish mine at Kiruna.

24 February 2016

NSB Class BM 93 No. 58 is seen at Andalsnes in snowy conditions as passengers board for the journey to Dombas, which will take this diesel multiple unit along the amazing and stunning Rauma Railway.

3 March 2019

Railcare Class 185 Nos 413 and 411 arrive double-headed into Narvik with a rake of loaded iron ore wagons. These locomotives are ex-Rush Rail and are now on hire to Railcare from BURE Equity.

3 March 2019

LKAB Class IORE twin unit Nos 106 and 134 run through Narvik with a lengthy rake of empty iron ore wagons. All IORE locomotives carry names: 106 is named *Kiruna*, which is the source of Swedish iron ore. 134 is named *Notviken*.

4 March 2019

LKAB Class IORE twin unit Nos 110 and 120 ease through Narvik with a rake of ore wagons heading back to Kiruna, which is the main source of Swedish iron ore. IORE locomotives are always coupled together to form a twin unit and are only uncoupled when one of the pair requires attention. 110 is named *Bjorkliden*, which is a station next to Tornetrask lake, and 120 is named *Kaisepakte*, which is a mountain overlooking the same lake.

2 March 2019

LKAB Class IORE twin unit Nos 111 and 133 are seen in fading light preparing to reverse a rake of ore wagons back into the stabling sidings of the LKAB unloading facility at Narvik. These locomotives are among the most powerful in the world. 111 is named *Katterat*, which is a remote station on the line, and 133 is named *Kopparasen*.

4 March 2019

LKAB Class IORE twin unit Nos 122 and 129 trundle through Narvik with a rake of empty ore wagons. Narvik, due to its deep-water year-round ice-free fjord, is perfect for LKAB to load ocean tankers with ore destined for all over the world. 122 is named *Ratsi*, which is a rail junction south of Kiruna, and 129 is named *Nattavaara*, which is a station south of Gallivare.

4 March 2019

Green Cargo Class Rc4 No. 1308 blasts through Narvik with a rake of cargo wagons during a period of intense activity at the station. As 1308 arrives an IORE is departing back to Kiruna with a rake of ore wagons and on the right a piece of on-track plant that has stopped to clear the way for the Rc4 can just about be made out.

5 March 2019

SJ Class Rc6 No. 1401 is enveloped in a snowstorm while passengers board the daily night train No. 93, which goes from Narvik to Stockholm. Any locomotive that travels this route in winter needs to be built to withstand the harsh conditions, with temperatures dropping to 40 degrees below freezing.

3 March 2019

Three T Class TMZ No. 1405 is seen at Narvik shunting a rake of empty log wagons just after a night of fresh snow.

2 March 2019

Bane NOR Class snow machine is seen having just descended into Narvik after completing the daily snow clearance duties on the iron ore line that runs from the mine of Kiruna to the offloading point at Narvik.

4 March 2019

Bane NOR Class track vehicle has just arrived at Narvik and pulled into the platform to allow a Green Cargo Rc4 to have the line so it can access the port of Narvik. This track vehicle is seen hauling a mobile work cabin that appears to be a converted shipping container.

Slovakia

Slovakia has a rail network of roughly 2,250 miles, and just over 980 miles have been electrified. The network includes some 75 tunnels and 2,321 bridges. The national operator here is ZSSK, with its freight division being ZSSK Cargo and infrastructure care division being ZSR. Between the various divisions of passenger, freight and infrastructure, a staggering variety of traction is used with locomotives that first entered service in the 1960s working alongside modern types such as Vectrons and Skoda 109s, which were introduced in 2012. Slovakia sees lots of cross-border freight and passenger workings and the country is a key artery for Continental rail travel.

15 February 2020

ZSSK Class 110 No. 034 is found stabled at Kosice while between shunting duties. This class is very rare indeed, with only two of the fifty examples used by the company still in active service.

14 February 2020

ZSSK Class 240 No. 098 is at Bratislava Hlavna Stanica picking up passengers with a rake of double-decked carriages. No. 098 is looking a bit work-stained and could do with a clean and a fresh coat of paint, but this view does show the cross-arm pantograph carried by the 240 fleet.

14 February 2020

ZSSK Class 263 No. 010 is seen at Bratislava Hlavna Stanica making a station call to pick up and set down passengers using a rake of double-deck carriages. No. 010 is displaying the standard ZSSK livery as applied to almost all ZSSK locomotives and units.

14 February 2020

ZSSK Class 350 No. 007 is seen in the early evening at Bratislava Hlavna Stanica with an express passenger working. No. 007 is displaying an advertising livery for the previous year's world ice hockey championship, which was won by Finland. The mascot for the games, named MACEJKO, can be seen on the loco's front end.

15 February 2020

ZSSK Class 362 No. 005 arrives at Bratislava Hlavna Stanica with a rake of single-deck passenger carriages, greeted by an almost empty station. The Class 362 is a dual-voltage type rebuilt from the older Class 363. The rebuild programme began in 2019.

13 February 2020

ZSSK Class 383 No. 102 prepares to depart from Bratislava Hlavna Stanica with a passenger working, having just backed onto its rake of single-deck carriages. The Class 383 all display this livery, which shows the ZSSK badge along with the Slovakian coat of arms and the words 'national carrier' in the centre.

15 February 2020

ZSSK Class 460 No. 029 is found at Kosice as passengers board. On the rear is classmate No. 053. These electric multiple units are used on regional and commuter services around Kosice.

15 February 2020

ZSSK Class 671 No. 005 is seen at Kosice with a passenger working to Cierna nad Tisou, which is a town in the Kosice region near the Tisa river. The Class 671 is a double-decked electric multiple unit that is very similar to the Czech Class 471.

15 February 2020

ZSSK Class 721 No. 102 is seen at Kosice acting as station pilot having just completed another empty coaching stock move. No. 102 will now pull out of the station and reverse onto another rake of coaching stock that has just arrived and will take those coaches for cleaning. No. 102 is displaying a very colourful if slightly worn livery.

15 February 2020

ZSSK Class 754 No. 004 is seen at Kosice in the late afternoon sun having just brought the author to the end of a six-hour journey from Bratislava. These big diesels are a common sight all over Eastern Europe and are operated by both national and open access passenger and freight companies.

15 February 2020

ZSSK Class 757 No. 023 catches the last rays of sun at Kosice as it awaits departure with a rake of single-deck passenger carriages. The Class 757 varies from the Class 754 as it is slightly more powerful and has a greater tractive effort. This class was also rebuilt from the old Class 750 between 2010 and 2015.

13 February 2020

ZSSK Cargo Class 240 No. 088 has just arrived at Bratislava Hlavna Stanica while on passenger duty with a rake of single-deck carriages. No. 088 is displaying a heavily work-stained and weathered ZSSK Cargo livery, although the identification plate on the front appears to have recently been painted.

15 February 2020

ZSSK Cargo Class 746 No. 015 is seen deep in the freight yard at Kosice while on shunting duty with a rake of tanker wagons. The Class 746 were purchased second-hand from the Czech Republic and were rebuilt between 2009 and 2011.

13 February 2020

ZSR Class MVTV 02 No. 04 is found stabled at Bratislava Hlavna Stanica along with classmate No. 09, which is behind but out of shot. The role of the MVTV 02 fleet is that of overhead line equipment maintenance. They are based on heavily modified Class 810 DMUs.

14 February 2020

LokoTrain Class 193 No. 222 Is seen at Bratislava Hlavna Stanica having stopped for a red signal with a long rake of loaded log wagons. 222 has been on hire to LokoTrain from Ell since 2015 and was even sub-hired out to Regiojet for around six months.

14 February 2020

PSZ Class 242 No. 262 and Class 468 No. 002 make for an interesting double-headed combination as they rumble through Bratislava Hlavna Stanica with a rake of grain wagons. PSZ own a very varied fleet of locomotives and these two classes are pretty rare, with only four Class 242 owned by PSZ along with this sole example of Class 468.

14 February 2020

Ceske drahy Class 380 No. 015 is seen late in the evening as darkness begins to fall at Bratislava Hlavna Stanica. It is powering an international passenger working that started in the Czech Republic and is going to Hungary via Slovakia.

14 February 2020

Regiojet Class 386 No. 203 is seen at Bratislava Hlavna Stanica with a daily cross-border working to Prague in the Czech Republic. No. 203 looks very smart indeed in the standard Regiojet livery.

14 February 2020

OBB Class 2016 No. 095 has just pulled into Bratislava Hlavna Stanica with a mixed rake of passenger carriages consisting of ZSSK and OBB city shuttle coaches. Class 2016 is the same as the ER Class operated by Regiojet, both types being part of the Eurorunner series.

13 February 2020

Regiojet Class ER-20 No. 011 makes for an impressive sight as it pulls away from Bratislava Hlavna Stanica with a rake of double-deck carriages. Regiojet has only two Class ERs in its fleet and both are on hire from Beacon Rail and used on the Bratislava-Komarno route. The ER stands for Eurorunner.

Slovenia

Like its neighbour Croatia, when the break-up of Yugoslavia began Slovenia found its rail connections severed by war. The Slovenian network is currently around 730 miles, and around half of this is electrified. The national operator here is SZ, which operates an intriguing mix of imported traction such as the Class 363 from France and the Class 541 and 312 built by Siemens. With a domestic network connecting most major towns and cities and numerous international routes, Slovenia has become more important to Continental freight and passenger services.

19 July 2018

SZ Class 310 No. 001 is found at Ljubljana having just arrived on a warm summer's day as passengers board with a service to Maribor.

19 July 2018

SZ Class 342 No. 001 is seen at Ljubljana on passenger duty with a rake of single-deck carriages. Class 342s are found on passenger workings which consist of either express or regional diagrams. Forty were built, but only nine are left.

19 July 2018

SZ Class 541-0 No. 011 pulls out of the freight yard just beyond Ljubljana station and rumbles slowly into the station with a rake of empty scrap wagons. The Class 541 belongs to the Eurosprinter family of locomotives and are a triple-voltage variant for working into Austria, Croatia and Germany.

19 July 2018

SZ Class 541-1 No. 108 is seen at Ljubljana having just pulled into the station on a light engine move. Once an intermodal train hauled by classmate 105 has passed, it will reverse back into the yard and await its next turn of duty.

19 July 2018

SZ Class 643 No. 026 is found stabled at Ljubljana station while between duties. These locomotives are used on shunting and also light freight diagrams. Twenty-three of the fifty built are still in operation.

19 July 2018

SZ Class 711 No. 015 is seen under the station canopy at Ljubljana on an incredibly hot day while between passenger duties. This class of diesel multiple units is used on long-distance regional services.

19 July 2018

SZ Class 732 No. 194 is found stabled next to Ljubljana station while between shunting duties. These small diesel shunters can also be found working light freight diagrams, although this is rare as only three of the class remain in service.

Spain

Spain has four different rail gauges on its network of around 9,950 miles, of which roughly 6,300 is electrified. These gauges include broad, also known as Iberian gauge; standard; meter; and two narrow gauge. The national operator here is RENFE, which runs a wide variety of traction with the main long-distance types for loco-hauled services being the classes 252 and 334. The crowning jewel in the RENFE network is the high-speed AVE network, which is the largest and fastest high-speed network on the Continent. The classes 102 and 112, known as pato or duck due to their long sloping noses designs, are the most common types. Spain has very good cross-border connections to both France and Portugal that do not require changes of track gauge.

18 June 2017

RENFE Mercancias Class 253 Nos 015 and 072 are seen at Mora la Nova as the pair slow to stop for a red signal with a lengthy train of intermodal wagons. Sadly these fine locomotives are dirty and have been vandalised at some point.

18 June 2017

RENFE Mercancias Class 269 No. 353 is seen double-heading a short mixed freight with an unidentified classmate through Mora la Nova in the late afternoon sun. This is a scene that can no longer be witnessed as RENFE have withdrawn the class, and this pair were most likely cut up for scrap.

20 June 2017

RENFE Class 334 No. 022 is seen at the sleepy station of Balsicas-Mar Menor under a clear sunny sky with a passenger working heading to Barcelona. The Class 334 can be found on a huge variety of workings, from night trains to long-distance regional services.

19 June 2017

RENFE Class 440 No. 114 is seen under cloudy skies at Mora la Nova with a medium-distance passenger working. No. 114 would look very smart, were it not for the graffiti attack that is yet to be removed.

18 June 2017

RENFE Class 448 No. 011, seen with the mountains that follow the course of the River Ebro in the background, arrives at Mora la Nova with an express passenger service to Barcelona.

20 June 2017

RENFE Class 594 No. 007 waits to depart from Balsicas-Mar Menor with an express passenger service for which the class was built. The Class 594 are very similar to the Danish DSB ER and MF classes, but some carry a modernised front end.

20 June 2017

RENFE Class 599 No. 085 rests in the baking heat at Balsicas-Mar Menor while on a fast regional service in the Valencia region. These diesel multiple units were meant for broad gauge track but are fitted with standard variable gauge boogies instead.

18 June 2017
VIAS Rail Class ballast regulator is seen stabled next to Mora la Nova while between infrastructure workings. This ballast regulator was built by Plasser & Theurer and has seen plenty of use with VIAS Rail since its introduction, as can be seen by the amount of wear around the ballast shute.

Sweden

Sweden's rail network consists of around 9,300 miles of track, 5,000 miles of which is electrified. The national operator here is SJ, with the freight division being Green Cargo. The Rc family of electric locomotives form the backbone of freight and loco-hauled services with the Rc4 mainly on freight and the Rc6 on the loco-hauled diagrams. SJ passenger services are supplemented by the high-speed X2 electric trainsets, with the most common EMU being the Class X40. Sweden has several cross-border links to Norway and one to Denmark, including the iron ore line that links the mine at Kiruna with the deep-water ice-free port of Narvik. Here the IORE locos are king – even passenger services must give way to the all-important ore trains.

27 February 2019

SJ Class Rc6 No. 1348 is seen having just arrived at Uppsala with a passenger working from Stockholm. 1348 looks very smart in the standard SJ black livery, although a few of the Rc6 fleet do carry other liveries. These include the SSRT livery, which is silver and red.

7 March 2019

SJ Class Rc6 No. 1359 is seen early in the morning as the rain pours down at Stockholm Central with a passenger working consisting of single-deck carriages still carrying the previous blue livery, rather than the current SJ black livery.

2 March 2019

SJ Class Rc6 No. 1395 is seen at Kiruna in the snow with the previous evening's night train from Stockholm to Narvik. Kiruna is famous for being the site of the enormous iron ore mine that is owned by LKAB, which produces around 26.9 million tonnes of ore each year – all of which is transported by the IORE locomotives to Narvik or Lulea.

25 February 2019

SJ Class X2 No. 2014 is seen at Stockholm as passengers including the author board for the 8.25 service to Malmo. The Class X2 are the powercars that, with a DVT at the other end, make up the high-speed electric trainsets.

26 February 2019

SJ Class X2 No. 2018 is seen at Goteborg waiting to depart back to Stockholm with the 17.29 service. The Class X2 are only ever seen working within Sweden, where they can use their tilting capabilities to the full.

25 February 2019

SJ Class X40 No. 3323 is seen at Malmo in the early evening just as the sun begins to set. The Class X40 is a double-decked electric multiple unit and comes in two- or three-car variants and can be found throughout Sweden on local services.

27 February 2019

SJ Class X55 No. 3763 has just arrived at Uppsala with a passenger working from Stockholm. The X55 Class of electric multiple units are very similar to the SJ Class X52 as both are from the Regina family of units.

27 February 2019

Green Cargo Class Rc4 No. 1188 races through Uppsala with a rake of fully loaded intermodal wagons. Green Cargo is the freight division of SJ and operates a number of freight types, but the Rc4 is by far the most common.

25 February 2019

Green Cargo Class V5 No. 152 is found stabled at Malmo yard while between duties, with a Snalltaget Class 193 Vectron locomotive for company. These diesel shunters are kept busy most of the time either shunting empty coaching stock or sorting out freight wagons.

25 February 2019

Snalltaget Class 193 No. 254 is seen stabled in the Malmo rail yard along with a rake of Snalltaget carriages while between workings. Snalltaget run passenger services between Malmo and Stockholm, as well as, in the summer months, a night train from Malmo to Berlin.

25 February 2019

Infranord Class LMV No. 0955 is found stabled at Malmo rail yard tucked away in a quiet corner. The Infranord Class LMV is used as a catenary maintenance vehicle and replaced some of the older types in the same role.

26 February 2019

TAGAB Class Rc3 No. 1063 is at Goteborg with a rake of single-deck carriages for the Goteborg to Karlstad service on which the fleet of five TAGAB Rc3 locomotives operate. TAGAB operate a varied and historic fleet of diesel and electric locomotives.

27 February 2019

UppTaget Class X11 No. 3137 rests at Uppsala while waiting to depart with the 13.41 service No 8514, which will run to Sala. UppTaget use three of these electric multiple units, which are on loan from Krosatagen.

27 February 2019

UppTaget Class X52 No. 9052 is about to depart from Uppsala on a cloudy morning. The Class X52 is by far the most common type of traction operated by UppTaget, with a fleet totalling ten units.

27 February 2019

SL Class X60 No. 6035 is seen at Uppsala waiting to depart with a working to Arlanda Sodertalje that is going via Stockholm. These electric multiple units normally work in pairs and work the Stockholm commuter routes.

Switzerland

Due to its location on the Continent, you could say Switzerland, with its network of some 3,300 miles (99 per cent electrified), could be seen as the beating heart of the Continental rail network. The national operator here is SBB, which operates a vast fleet of locomotives and multiple units alongside some very sleek high-speed trainsets. Alongside the standard gauge network there are several narrow gauge lines, with the biggest and best-known operator being RhB, which has a vast network in the south-east of the country. Switzerland enjoys several cross-border links to its neighbouring countries.

15 September 2019

SBB Class Ee 922 No. 022 is seen under a clear blue September sky at Basel coupled up to a rake of single-deck carriages and a DVT waiting to take them for cleaning. These electric shunters are found at most major Swiss stations.

20 February 2020

SBB Class RABDe 500 No. 021 is seen at Zurich having just arrived at the end of its journey. The RABDe 500 Class are used on high-speed inter-city workings and have the ability to tilt, allowing them to take curves faster. 021 carries the name *Jeremias Gotthelf*, who was a well-known Swiss novelist.

22 September 2019

SBB Class RABDe 502 No. 011 is found at Basel with the inter-city 3 service to Chur that will go via Zurich and Landquart. This class of double-deck electric trainsets are built for express inter-city workings and have a passive tilt ability. No. 011 carries the name and coat of arms for *Romanshorn*, which is a municipality located in the canton of Thurgau.

20 February 2020

SBB Class Re 420 No. 11130 rests at the buffers having just brought in a NightJet service to Zurich. The Class Re 420 fleet of electric locomotives are used on a variety of passenger-hauled loco services normally based around Euro and inter-city services, plus regional and night train diagrams.

21 September 2019

SBB Class Re 460 No. 030 is seen at Brig with a rake of single-deck carriages, with the Swiss Alps making for a spectacular backdrop. The Re 460 Class are the fastest electric locomotives used on passenger services. No. 030 carries the name *Santis*, which is a mountain located in north-eastern Switzerland.

20 February 2020

SBB Class Re 460 No. 080 is seen at Zurich with a rake of double-decked carriages. The Re 460 Class are only used on inter-city and inter-regional passenger diagrams throughout Switzerland. No. 080 is seen displaying the advertising livery for Migros, which is Switzerland's biggest retail company.

16 September 2019

Rhatische Bahn Class ABe 8/12 No. 3513 is found at St Moritz and is about to depart with its next working. This class of dual-voltage electric multiple units are found on services throughout the RhB network. All of the class carry names, with 3513 being named *Simeon Bavier*, who was a Swiss politician.

25 July 2015

Rhatische Bahn Class Ge 3/3 No. 215 is found stabled at Chur while between shunting duties. Only two of these electric shunters were built, with one being based at Chur and the other being based at Samedan. These shunters are typically used for shunting empty coaching stock.

21 September 2019

Rhatische Bahn Class Ge 4/4 II No. 620 is at Chur making a passenger stop while working a glacier express train to Disentis, which will then be taken onwards to Brig and finally Zermatt. 620 is carrying a promotional livery for the RhB Club and carries the name and coat of arms for *Zernez*, which is a town located in Graubunden canton.

20 September 2017

Rhatische Bahn Class Ge 4/4 II No. 629 is seen at Disentis having just taken over a glacier express working, and will power the working to Chur. 629 carries the name and coat of arms of *Tiefencastel*, which is a village in the Graubunden canton. This loco carries an advertising livery for the new Abula tunnel.

16 September 2019

Rhatische Bahn Class Ge 4/4 III No. 642 is seen at St Moritz having just arrived with a passenger working, which includes a historic carriage that is coupled up behind 642. All of the Ge 4/4 III fleet carry special liveries and names. 642 carries the advertising livery for Integral, which is a Swiss pension schemes company. The name carried by this loco is *Briel/Brigels*, which is a municipality in the Graubunden canton.

18 September 2019

Rhatische Bahn Class Ge 4/4 III No. 652 is seen at Davos and is interestingly coupled between two rakes of passenger carriages, with a classmate leading from the other end. 652 carries the name and coat of arms for *Vaz/Obervaz* and *Lenzerheide-Valbella*. *Vaz/Obervaz* is a municipality and Lenzerheide-Valbella is a village, both being located in the Graubunden canton. No. 652 carries the promotional livery for the hockey club Davos.

18 September 2019

Rhatische Bahn Class Ge 6/6 I No. 414 is seen at Filisur while working a RhB historic train, which consists of historic and open viewing wagons. No. 414 will now uncouple and run round its carriages before recoupling. This class once consisted of a fifteen-strong fleet, but nowadays only two are operational. Four in museums and the other nine were scrapped. The class were nicknamed 'Crocodile'.

19 September 2019

Rhatische Bahn Class Ge 6/6 II No. 703 is seen as darkness begins to fall at Tiefencastel with a rake of mixed freight. This class is made up of a seven-strong fleet and all are named. 703 is named and carries the coat of arms for the mountain town of St Moritz, located in the Graubunden canton.

17 September 2019

Rhatische Bahn Class Ge 6/6 II No. 705 is seen at Samedan waiting for the signal to proceed with a rake of logs. The Class Ge 6/6 II are used for hauling the freight trains over the RhB network. 705 carries the name and coat of arms for *Pontresina/ Puntraschigna*, which is a municipality in the canton of Graubunden.

21 September 2019

Rhatische Bahn Class Tm 2/2 No. 25 is found at Disentis while stabled between shunting duties. These diesel shunters can be found all over the RhB network, normally tucked away somewhere quiet or stabled at a station.

20 September 2019

Rhatische Bahn Class Tm 2/2 No. 83 is seen stabled at Bergun while between infrastructure duties and is coupled up to a loaded wagon full of equipment. This version of the Tm 2/2 varies from the previous one; it is reserved for infrastructure duties and carries the yellow livery to denote this role.

20 February 2020

OBB Class 1116 No. 202 is seen at Zurich with a Railjet service. The locomotive and its carriages will continue to Prague. This is possible due to the class being duel-voltage.

18 September 2019

WRS Class ES 64 U2 No. 100 is seen stabled while between freight duties and is waiting at Landquart for its next diagram to begin. This locomotive has been hired out to no fewer than six operators since it was built in 2000 and entered service with WRS in January 2019.

20 September 2017

MGB Class Deh 4/4 I No. 24 is seen at Disentis having just coupled up to a MGB passenger working that is heading towards Zermatt. A loco change is required here due to the need for a locomotive fitted with a rack and pinion to get the services over the steep inclines. No. 24 carries the name and coat of arms for Tasch, which is a municipality in the Valais canton.

20 September 2017

MGB Class HGe 4/4 II No. 3 is seen at Disentis having just uncoupled and having performed a reversing move to clear the line for a RhB Ge 4/4 II to take over the glacier express working it has just brought in. No. 3 carries the name *Dom*, which is the third highest mountain in the Alps.

21 September 2019

BLS Cargo Class Re 485 No. 004 rumbles through Brig with a rolling highway train, which is conveying heavy goods vehicles and their drivers by rail between countries. These workings save the lorries a long and potentially dangerous route over the Alps.

21 September 2019

BLS Cargo Class Re 485 No. 019 is seen passing slowly through Brig light engine while on its way to the BLS locomotive depot next to the station. No. 019 will then couple up to a classmate, which will be hauled dead in tow to its destination.